The author has an intensive passion for creativity, innovation and motivation while his leadership experiences also acts as a bonus for him in various areas. He strongly believes in coaching people to become great in life and has not only lived through the principles in this book but has equally practiced the action points therein, and it's in the application of these principles that make one not only enjoy his/her life as a person but will also influence others around you to think about living positively.

Recommendation: "Every human being is a unique individual who develops their own version of success and achievement. In this book Temitayo Oyediran shows us, step-by-step, how we can move forward to reach our goals."
– By Kathy Ennis (Founder &
MD of Envision Impression
Management Ltd).

SELF-IDENTIFICATION MANAGEMENT
(SIM)

Handbook on how to manage your Self Identity.
Learn to know more, become more and to give more.

TEMITAYO OYEDIRAN

authorHOUSE®

AuthorHouse™ UK
1663 Liberty Drive
Bloomington, IN 47403 USA
www.authorhouse.co.uk
Phone: 0800.197.4150

Published by AuthorHouse 09/12/2016

ISBN: 978-1-5246-3708-8 (sc)
ISBN: 978-1-5246-3706-4 (hc)
ISBN: 978-1-5246-3707-1 (e)

Print information available on the last page.

CONTENTS

FOREWORD

Self Identification Management System is not just another book; it is a tool for self-discovery and self-mastery. Temitayo has masterfully put together a well-researched and resourceful manual filled with applicable guides on how to be in sync with ones innermost being. The author clearly demonstrates that It is by finding the 'you' in you that you are able to conquer personal barriers and also unleash the hidden treasure locked up within your spirit. This system of knowledge is both developmental and transformational.

I recommend this book to all who want to break beyond the threshold of seeming limitations to the empowering pedestal of internal possibilities hidden in us by God. My prayer goes with this work that the reader will find the understanding of what it means to enjoy the abundant life.

Dr Morakinyo Olumodimu
Linguistics Department
Tulane University
New Orleans, USA

PREFACE

I can liken this self-identification manual to a farmer who plants a seed and nurtures it to germinate and become a tree that will bear fruits that can feed many people. A life that is well lived is a life that is properly understood and managed diligently to deliver effective results.

I have often heard it said – "you'll literally be seen in everything or about anything that you do or you're engaged in." What that means is that people can partially see you or reflect your personality in all that you do: be it your education, career, leadership role, ministerial duties, family, friends or associates, your area of interest, course of study, business and virtually anything you might decide to engage in. It is also said that people can easily perceive the kind of person you are by merely reading or hearing about what you do. If this is possible, then why would we not mind spending more time identifying ourselves and managing our identity, so that people will only see what we want them to see in us because that is truly who we are. I've personally been through the process of trying to understand myself, so I know how frustrating it can get.

I can be sure that many things about you in general do not make any sense (to you) as to why they happen; at times you may try to ignore them but when the same issue keeps recurring, you might want to find out what's going on; in the process, you begin to discover who you truly are and what exactly is your identity. It's at this stage that you'll be able to unravel some hidden truths about yourself that no one has ever told you of or would ever have told you; not because they don't want you to know, but because they don't know the answers to the issues, except you're able to figure it out yourself. With this mindset, you begin to ask yourself numerous questions such as how to start searching for your own identity, and, when you find it, how do you manage it effectively.

These are some of the questions that the SIM handbook steers us through, with steps, processes and action plans that we can apply to effectively manage our self-identity in order to achieve our ordained purpose here on earth.

ABBREVIATIONS

CSSF - Critical Self-Success Factor

SA – Self Analysis

SC – Self Control

SI – Self Identification

SIM – Self Identification Management

SIP – Self Identification Plan

SM – Self Management

ACKNOWLEDGEMENTS

I want to take this opportunity to thank those people who, through their kind gestures, have helped me to start and to complete this book through their inspiration, financial and moral support, advice and encouragement. I believe that without these people and without the help of God, SIM book would not have been a reality, as I've doubted myself so many times, but I just kept on believing that it would be possible one day if I just did not give up. I thank God for making this a success; and I thank everyone who has been part of this success. I also thank those who could have helped but were unable to do so; I want to say thanks to you as well, because I believe that you may be able to help in my next book.

Simon Jack is a friend like a brother who has always been there for me when I needed creative ideas for the SIM book or when I was stuck with how to proceed in organizing it. He constantly said things that encouraged me to try something new and it worked most of the time. Stuart Cowen (coach at VISA Europe) coached me when I needed someone to talk to concerning how to structure my plans in order to achieve my goals in life and to impact on other lives around me.

Sincere gratitude goes to my amazing family members: Mr & Mrs T O Oyediran (parents), Mrs Tolulope Lagbenro (younger sister), Mr Olusegun Oyediran (elder brother) and Mrs Ololade Olodude (elder sister), who had a great influence on me throughout my life and even until now. These people have supported me in making sure that I have become who I am today.

As a Christian, you have spiritual leaders who are always excited to see you doing great things and they are constantly praying for you to succeed in life; so I believe that I'm blessed to have Pastor Kayode and Pastor Mrs Ayo Fabiyi of Open Heavens Parish, Hatfield (RCCG) as exceptional spiritual leaders.

Mr Deji Adelegan is also a friend like a brother, who always ensures that I'm still passionate about fulfilling my purpose through writing inspirational articles and completing a work like this SIM book, which can inspire people to become more in life by doing more.

Kathy Ennis (personal coach and business mentor) did a wonderful job in helping me to figure out the right path/channel that I should take to ensure that I deliver a good message to people when I started writing this book.

And, to my future wife Bolanle Oyedokun (fiancée), who is always there to encourage me, even when I thought that I wasn't ready to get the book published, she literally pushed me into it. I want to say that I appreciate you since the day you came into my life. Thank you for being you and thanks for bringing out the best in me. At least this book is evidence of the many good things that you can still bring out of me.

Lastly, I want to say a big thank you to Edward A Dundon (editor), who provided insightful editing for this book. You've been so kind to me in editing this work and making it look real. To the many people out there, who have also encouraged me to write a book that they can read because they feel inspired each time I talk to them, I use this opportunity to also say thank you for your encouragement and I humbly present this piece of work to you now as you've requested it. I can assure you that as you read it, you will understand more about yourself in order to give more of yourself. Thank you all for your support.

OBJECTIVES OF SELF-IDENTIFICATION MANAGEMENT (SIM) PRACTICES

This self-identification manual is not just an ordinary book or series of texts that you must read in order to prosper in life. It is a tool that you must *plug* or *insert* into your life; and in doing so, it will enhance you to connect with other parts of yourself (i.e. self), so that you can launch into your own real being of fulfilling your maximum potential. Therefore, this information is necessary for everybody (especially not for the lazy ones with nonchalant attitudes); it is definitely for those who have come to terms with what they really need to understand about themselves so that they can understand and relate to other people. Self-awareness provides the opportunity of meeting with great potentials that can help people to enjoy great achievements and to fulfil their visions.

The main reason for putting this information together is for creating an awareness of how people can add value to themselves in order to deliver great value to others and their environment, simply by identifying their true 'self' and managing that 'self-identity'. Identification is the beginning of any development and without identifying a problem, one can never understand how to find the solution to that problem (i.e. from observation, one will be able to derive the solution to a problem and this is mostly found in the problem itself). Opportunities come through challenges or when people are being informed of challenges; however, they don't come in a way that is very obvious to everyone. Therefore, SIM depends on how prepared someone is to find out what the real problem is and identify the steps that should be taken in order to solve these problems.

DEFINITION OF SELF

Philosophers have agreed that the definition of self is the description of the being's essential qualities, which constitute a person's uniqueness or essential being. This means that self is the uniqueness of who you are and how you portray yourself to be.

The dictionary has many definitions of self and one is that self is 'a person's essential being that distinguishes them from others' (*New Oxford Dictionary of English*, 1998). Another definition is that self is one's personal interest, character or nature.

Psychologists, who have studied self, have come to the conclusion that self is the *cognitive* and *affective* representation of one's identity or the subject of a particular experience. They have also regarded self as playing an integral part in human motivation, cognition, affect, and social identity.

Buddhists also see self as the identification of our souls, minds, bodies and egos, while Christianity sees self as either true or false. Hence one can manifest both the true self and the false self, which is experienced when one commits a sin and moves away from the presence of God.

The above definitions are true to a degree, but I would love to define self as who you really are on the inside and that which emerges to reflection on the outside. Let me explain why I have come up with this definition.

If your mind has not been bolstered with the truth or if you're not exposed to the kind of inspiration that helps you to be identified with something good, you will not be thinking of doing good and no one will identify you with doing good. This is because you don't become good overnight, but you become good through the constant effort of being good to others. This is akin to borrowing money to your friend who needs it, just for the sake of expecting him or her to also lend you some money when you're in need. A person with morals does good to people without expecting those people to repay him or her with good deeds, although most people will naturally expect that, but it doesn't always happen like that.

There is this common phrase in my dialect that says "The day that a mad person identifies that he/she is mad, that means that the person is gradually recovering from madness or has finally recovered from being mad." In short, mad people are unaware of what they are doing and that is why they are termed as insane, but the moment that they're able to identify themselves as being mad, then they suddenly have come to terms with their madness; and, because no one would ordinarily want to be mad, they begin to ask people for help on how to recover from their instability. Although this is not a good example of describing how one should endeavour to identify oneself, it points out that everyone must inwardly search themselves, for who they truly are, before they venture into anything.

I have stated above that personality shows up in everything and in anything one does; therefore, people tend to see us through our company, professionalism, education, occupation, ministry, relationships, teams, family, organizations, leadership roles – virtually anything that we're engaged or featured in. If we're very much aware of this fact, then why don't we take more pleasure in searching ourselves more carefully, in order to begin to manage the understanding of who we are so that we can fully reap the benefits of actualizing our 'selves'?

The first step to success is *identification*. That is, identifying the problem or problems that can prevent you from becoming successful and the reasons why those problems exist. If you identify these issues and you understand why they exist, then your problem is half-solved; without identifying those problems, you might not get anywhere in trying to find the solution to a problem that you don't even know existed or where it originated from. This is where the SIM manual helps to understand those steps that you can take in order to actualize your dream, goal, ambition and purpose in life.

The dictionary defines self-identification as the act of identifying yourself as a particular kind of person. To buttress this definition, you need to understand why you are trying to identify yourself.

Self-identification is a reflective process where one thinks over the occurrence of events from previous/past experiences and considers the present circumstances in order to propose or project a splendid or magnificent future with great achievements. I classify self-identification as a form of analyzing ourselves in order to know the purpose and who we are really made to become in life, without which it is impossible to achieve anything. This can also help us to identify our strengths and weaknesses, which may be handy in measuring up to what we can achieve and what is it that can prevent or stop us from achieving those things, so that we can quickly address them and move on. If we do not understand what our main purpose is in life, we will only be influenced or carried away by what we can see around us or what other people are doing (nowadays, especially the celebrities and famous people) without truly understanding why they did what they did before they became who they have become. I would like to point out that it is essentially different *knowing* our purpose in life than *understanding* our purpose in life. The two of them differ from each other and I will briefly explain why this is so. We would all agree that knowledge is an act of gathering truth or information about something, while understanding is also the act of deep knowledge about something, but it is better to understand something than merely know that it exists.

When you have knowledge about something, you scratch the surface to know it; understanding something, on the other hand, makes you dig through the facts and figures of your findings and that alone will greatly reveal more truths about the issue. This goes beyond simply knowing that you understand how, where and when to apply the knowledge.

Knowing yourself means that you know your strengths, weaknesses, habits, feelings, interests, and so on; however, understanding yourself means that you know and understand why they are your strengths, weaknesses and so on. Understanding helps you to know more, rather than scratching the surface. It provides deeper understanding and perspectives of who you are and why you must do what you ought to do in order to achieve what you intend to achieve. Self-knowledge sometimes concern studies, findings and experiences about yourself, but understanding involves deeper research and self-analysis; so if you must fulfil your purpose in life then you must identify what your purpose is and begin to manage yourself to the point of actualizing that purpose.

If you're very much aware of your purpose in life, you won't be at ease with yourself until the goals you have set are achieved. It's not only achievement alone that matters but also the maintenance of such an achievement because your goals can serve a lot of people and remain for a very long time, even after you're dead. Being at ease when you have a goal to achieve means that you are not so passionate in fulfilling that dream and you are unlikely to eventually fulfil it. (I will expatiate more on passion in another chapter of this manual.) As a man or woman with so much passion, when things are not going the way you've envisioned, I believe that you will never be at rest. You can't just keep calm, even though people around you may not be able to see what you can see unless you can reveal it to them; additionally, they may not be able to see it exactly how you can see it and this may make you want to be in control of the process of actualizing that dream; therefore, it is necessary for you to manage those steps that you've identified as the necessary ways that can take you to your end goal in life.

Let me quickly brief you about my own story on how I was able to identify my real self; features of which still look very strange to some people who knew me then. When they see me now, they are baffled by what I have suddenly become. I still try to maintain myself, but do things differently because I know better now. I will skip much of the early part of the story and quickly go to the part when I failed some courses during my first year at Babcock University in Nigeria, where I was studying for my BSc in Computer Science (Technology). I failed these courses not because I didn't prepare at all for the exams, or maybe I didn't read but because I always used to read only to pass an exam and not prepare ahead for exams. I would only read what I felt comfortable with reading and hoped that the lecturer would not bring out those parts of the notes which I didn't read or understand. This was what happened until I got my first year's results and I realized that I had failed three courses and would have to return to summer school during the holidays, or wait to retake the courses during the normal session, which would be an additional burden on me because of the normal modules scheduled for my second year.

My parents and supervisors advised me to retake the courses, so I decided to attend the summer school when most students were on holidays. It was during this summer school that I realized that I was only fooling myself by reading what I felt like reading and ignoring that part of the course that I was not comfortable with. When I started this summer session, I noticed that many students who were not that serious about their studies during the school session did not come to the summer school, which meant that they either passed all their courses or postponed the re-sit for their failed courses till later year(s). Then I asked myself why would I want to use my school session to read (for only what I felt like reading in preparation for an exam) and then return in the summer to still continue to read when I was supposed to be at home enjoying my holidays with friends and family.

I remember sitting down on my bed in one of those days and promising myself that I would do everything possible not to return to summer school again, even if it meant that I would stretch myself to do additional reading that would qualify me to pass my courses. During the time that I was still sitting down on my bed, I also remember that another motivation for me to read well for my studies was the promise that my dad gave me when I was growing up; he reminded me of that same promise again when I got to Babcock: that he would sponsor me to do my master's degree in the United Kingdom if I could only emerge with nothing less than a second class upper (2.1) grade in my bachelor's degree. I kept these words to myself, as well as the promises that I made when I went for summer school and they lasted until I eventually graduated from Babcock University with a second class upper (2.1). In addition, I already had an invitation to study at the University of Hertfordshire in the United Kingdom, while I was still writing my final year project for my first degree.

Why am I sharing this sensational story with you? It is to tell you that I had to identify what I needed in my life before I could actually achieve anything in life; the achievement of my BSc kept me going in other areas of my life, one of which was that I decided I wanted to write a book. I now started researching the material that people include in successful and saleable books. Reading more books motivated me to do what I wanted to do, which is to become an author of book(s). I became interested in following John C. Maxwell, because I liked his style of writing. I also became interested in reading business books and listening to audio books from people like Richard Branson, Daniel Priestley, Pastor E A Adeboye, Abraham Maslow, Napoleon Hill, T D Jakes, President

Barack Obama, Robert Kesley, Zig Ziglar, Brain Tracy and Jim Rohn. I also followed many of these speakers and writers on social media networks, so that I could tap into their wealth of knowledge and wisdom. I very much read the Bible constantly in order to get some inspirations and revelations, which brings about more wisdom.

MANAGEMENT

Management is generally defined as the planning and controlling of every activity or process involved in achieving a desired goal. If that is correct, then the management of self-identity could also be described as following the steps that help to control the activities surrounding the understanding of who we are and the purpose(s) that we're meant to achieve.

Management is an act of setting a plan and ensuring that the plan is sequentially or randomly adhered to by people who are responsible for implementing the plan.

The issue of managing yourself is the ultimate of all other forms of management that are under discussion, because you can simply achieve nothing without managing yourself to the point of fulfilling any goal in life. It is simply impossible to manage any other thing without first managing yourself: be it your business, project, event, team or employees. In fact, it is essential that every management task or obligation is supported by a plan of action that can record or keep track of the progress of every activity in the management process: how, for instance, can one do a task without identifying the requirements of the management tasks involved? These must be included in the progress report of whatever one tries to manage.

There is a phrase that states *"Nothing else works unless you work something."* It is absolutely necessary that we work out the way we want to manage ourselves or our strengths, as these endeavours are useful in fulfilling the purpose why we've identified them as our strengths. For example, the time on the clock cannot be controlled to either go faster or slower than normal; on the other hand, we can easily adjust ourselves in order to make the time work in our favour. Then we can say that self-management supersedes time management because we can manage ourselves to make the time work for our advantage. We cannot, however, manipulate the time in order that it can serve us alone; because time is relatively the same in any regional location).

CHARACTERISTICS OF SIM: WHO ARE YOU?

Human beings have many characteristics that make them different from other species; these characteristics, however, are different from what makes an individual understand himself or herself. Here is a brief explanation of a question that people may be asked about who they are and how to understand certain things about themselves. These features provide an overview of what people expect to see in us; hence, giving them a feeling that we actually understand the above question – who are you?

- *Self-discipline* – This is actually one of the most critical aspects of SIM because it cuts across all other characteristics or features of self: be it self-image, self-development or self-awareness. You cannot achieve anything without self-discipline and neither can you achieve any other aspect of self if you're not disciplined. It also involves setting some boundaries and targets for yourself, with some metrics in place to measure how far you have progressed in developing yourself. There's no self-development without self-discipline and this must be measured in relation to the success of the processes in self-development, otherwise there wouldn't be SIM. This is a characteristic that involves some form of training that would mean you go through some scrutiny of options and narrow down your options to stream down the most valuable behaviour or resources for the growth of the self

"A man without decision of character can never be said to belong to himself.... He belongs to whatever can make captive of him." (Quotes on self-discipline, 1996–2013)

And, another quote on self-discipline:

"Self-discipline is a form of freedom. Freedom from laziness and lethargy, freedom from expectations and demands of others, freedom from weaknesses and fear or doubt. Self-discipline allows a pitcher to feel his individuality, his inner strength, his talent. He is master of, rather than a slave to, his thoughts and emotions."

(Dorfman, 2002, pp. 24, 91)

When we talk of discipline, we tend to believe that it must only be done to other people (i.e. subordinates); sometimes, however, we need to subject ourselves to some rules that we must individually set for ourselves and then work rigorously to adhere to these rules.

The only major difference with this kind of discipline is that no one will punish you for not abiding by the set rules of self-discipline, except you personally attach some punishments to it, which means that you will have to think twice before you go beyond the boundary or disobey the rules you set for yourself.

While thinking of self-discipline, I thought of this as a quote and this has actually helped me in identifying so many things about myself; the quote has made me believe that I can achieve anything if I can discipline myself and work towards it: *"Discipline is not negotiable. You either get better through self-discipline or somebody/something somewhere will somehow discipline you."*

(Oyediran, 2014)

- *Self-image* – This is the kind of image that puts you in front of others so that they tend to treat you like that. It is the way you have conceptualized yourself to be and it affects how you display yourself to people around you, with the attitude that you give to things that you find yourself doing. This goes to say that you will be addressed the way you portray yourself to people. Your image is a representation of who you present yourself to be to them, even if you're not right there in front of them then: as long as they can see your image, they can begin to assume you're the kind of person that you are.

- *Self-development* – This is the act of growing yourself for the benefit of increasing certain things or behaviours that can propel you to a greater height, make you look more professional or give your self-image a boost. Development is a gradual process and it takes a lot of commitment to fully attain a self-developed level in the stages of your personal growth. This act is achieved by progressing in the way you do things or the manner in which you appear to people, which indirectly tells people that you're no longer the same person they saw the last time they observed you. To be self-developed is to have progressed to a higher level of achievement that is better and bigger than in a previous situation. The sort of achievements from self-development could be in different forms such as behavioural, career, intellectual, status and so on.

Lao-tzu, one of the greatest philosophers and poets of ancient China, wrote: *"Mastering others is strength, but mastering yourself is true power."*

- *Self-control* – Many gadgets and devices cannot be operated properly or correctly without remote controls. Control is a powerful word and it must be present in the life of every one of us, if we truly want to go far in life. When we have control over ourselves, we tend to know where we should go and what we should do without going beyond the control that we've placed on ourselves. Control is what tells us what to do and when to do it. It is responsible for restraining us from certain things that our body system will normally crave for; although we have self-control, we dare not do these things because we know that they are not good for us. Until we induce ourselves with self-control, we cannot begin to deal with self-development and SIM would be far from been achieved. In the same way that we cannot operate some features of a TV, CD/video player and skybox decoders without using the remote control, so also it may be very difficult to fully understand ourselves or achieve a lot without implementing self-control. It's just like a button that we'd use to put ourselves in order, eventually leading to the so-called perfect man or woman.

Aristotle, one of the greatest scientists and Greek philosophers, stated this in a quote: *"We are what we repeatedly do; excellence then is not an act but a habit."*

It is possible to set a boundary for ourselves and for a higher authority to set a boundary for us, in which we are not allowed to cross over these boundaries. Having control over yourself so that you are able to do everything rather than crossing that boundary may be described as having self-control; this phenomenon is not very common now when people just do whatever they like because they feel that way.

In the case of a child whose father tells him or her not to do something and he or she goes ahead to do that thing repeatedly without any remorse, it may be said of that child that he or she lacks self-control; additionally, someone may set a personal boundary where he or she wants to desist from doing certain bad things.

It may be very difficult to yield to that but if you can control your urge(s) for these things, it will be clear that you have self-control to stay away from the thing that you don't want to do; consequently, people will respect you for that.

Put simply, self-control affects what we decide to do for ourselves; in return, we gain people's respect and confidence and we can achieve anything because we possess an attitude of self-control.

- *Self-management* – This is responsible for the direction, administration and control of the self to fully deliver the necessary potentials in oneself for an available responsibility, such as to achieve a calculated goal. In managing one's self, principles and steps must be followed so that they can lead us directly to the target or our goal(s). If self-management is not done with great concentration, it can lead to self-destruction which invariably means self-mismanagement. Many factors need to be considered when discussing self-management, but that is not the main focus of this book. We will discuss a few other characteristics of self, which may help us to break down what SIM is all about and how it came about.

It has been said: "*It is not enough to have great qualities; we should also have the management of them.*" (La Rochefoucauld, 1900)

- *Self-worth* – Worth is the value of a substance and because value cannot be measured; it may only be accepted by how you present it to others. This is an act of nurturing one's self in a valuable manner, such that people will be glad to support your cause of action.

Worth is a result of the price that you place on yourself – for people to actually consider contacting you to solve their problems for them or advise them on what they should do in difficult situations. If your self-worth is not properly considered and analysed, it would not add any profit to the gift or talents that you've been endowed with.

Therefore, one needs to understand their worth and place great value on this entity. This is one of the most important fundamentals of fully identifying one's self, because this is where you can actually enrich yourself through the potentials that you have within you; however, this should not be categorized or classified as self-ego because you do not have to be an egoist before you can possess self-worth.

- *Self-confidence* – It takes a lot of courage to achieve so many things in life and courage can build confidence. Self-confidence doesn't mean that you are unafraid of anything or that you don't fear to fail; instead, it means that you have so much confidence in your ability to bounce back even when you fail, or that you're so confident in yourself that you can easily identify when you are in need and you're bold enough to easily ask for help when it is needed. This kind of confidence shows that you know what you're capable of doing and what you cannot do. And this confidence is built upon your awareness that there are some things that you can do exceptionally well and there are other things that you are not so good at; you are, however, only concentrating on those things that bring out the best in you for other people to appreciate and share with you. This kind of feeling can only be achieved when your self-confidence is on a higher level; and even if you don't know everything, you're still confident that you have enough knowledge that can get you out of trouble when you find yourself in any problem.

- *Self-indulgence* – It is possible to stay put and not want to face some challenges that can take you to your next level, considering that these challenges don't appear easy to bear.

(I've come to realize that most challenges that actually come our way are opportunities in disguise.) These challenges provide the opportunity for you to either face them while you learn something new or stay away from them and prevent yourself from learning vital lessons that the challenges bring. Just by looking at the problems, some people indulge themselves to stay away from such problems and that in itself will not rectify the situation; it will merely postpone or reserve the problems for later. When you return to these problems, they may have become more complicated. The best way to solve challenges is to carefully define the causes of these challenges by understanding them before looking for solutions. Indulging yourself in a luxurious lifestyle without investing in the future is not a wise thing to do because this enterprise involves a lot of planning, analyzing and management of yourself in order to fully enjoy your personal self-identification.

- *Self-awareness:* It takes a lot of discipline and dedication to know what you don't have, but it takes a lot of awareness to identify what you have. Self-awareness may be categorized as one of the features of self that reveals to you who you truly are by painting a picture of who you are to you, even if you never saw yourself like that. Being aware of yourself should precede the awareness of your environment or your awareness of your community or society. If you know your environment more than you know yourself, it will reflect in your attitude towards yourself and in what you deliver to your environment. It is your self-awareness that can have a positive impact on how much you know your environment and not the other way round. Your physical environment is an accumulation of species or people of different personalities; therefore, it is possible that your self-awareness can inspire someone within the same environment with you in order for them to identify their self-awareness and invariably impact their environment positively.

- *Self-government:* This is an understanding of how to govern yourself in order to fulfil your purpose. Governance is the art of taking authority over certain issues or if an authority is being delegated upon a person with the capability of disposing of it rightly. To govern yourself is to delegate authority to yourself so that you are independent and do not have to look at other people before you can execute judgement in most aspects of your life. All of us are governed by one being or the other and it is almost impossible for us to govern ourselves. This self-government aspect of self is not meant to confuse us; instead, it shows us a different aspect of self that we might not have being used to. We will not discuss too much about self-government in this book, but we must be aware that it is possible for one to govern his/her self; furthermore, it is a great advantage that we inhabit this trait of being independent to the point of governing ourselves.

- *Self-determination:* The decision to maintain a standardized way of living or whether to explore it deeply depends solely on different factors and one of these is self-determination. If you decide to live a healthy life or eat vegetarian meals, it must be for a purpose that should be backed up by self-determination, otherwise nothing will be achieved. A person can do research on the cause of certain problems and make decisions to change certain things that can provide a positive effect for that person. Such decisions can be carried through as a process of self-determination.

- *Self-esteem:* Esteem goes a long way to define who you are. If you are not sure of your self-esteem or you believe that you have low self-esteem, then that might be the reason why people trample upon you or descend on you as a nobody, who is not worthy to be reckoned with or of no value at all. There is a saying that says: "*respect is reciprocal*" and another that says "*you cannot give what you don't have*". This is the same thing as self-esteem because no one will respect you if you don't give yourself due respect; and, no one will expect any respect from you if it's obvious to them that you don't even respect yourself. An honourable person is one with a high self-esteem, while the one with a low self-esteem has no dignity at all.

- *Self-love:* According to my faith as a Christian, the Bible describes love as the greatest gift given to human beings. It is a gift because we can decide to give it to whoever we want to give it to. The Bible recommends that we should show love to everybody we encounter. If we are commanded to give love to anybody we come across, how then do we do this if we don't even show love to our 'self'? Self-love is the seed that must be sown in order to reap self-confidence, self-esteem and many other characteristics of self.

  If you do not genuinely love yourself, it will be very difficult to genuinely love others and it will be impossible for you to achieve anything great because you cannot afford the time it takes to identify the 'self', which you do not love.

- *Self-discovery*: Self-discovery symbolizes renewal, elicitation and it is borne out of sincere commitment to unravel mysteries about the self. Self-discovery is similar to re-birth; we don't, however, have to go back inside our mothers to be born all over again but we have to discover who we truly are. Let us bring life into it. For example, if a monkey is taken away from its mates in the jungle and placed in an environment where it will be treated like a normal human being (teaching it how to speak, cook, read, write and think like a human) and after a while, the animal is taken back into the jungle; it becomes a struggle for the monkey to re-adapt to its natural habitat because the monkey is now used to doing things like a normal human being. It will take a lot of hard work for the monkey to discover that it belongs to the ape world in the jungle; furthermore, it would have to re-adapt to the lifestyle of the other animals in the jungle in order to live life to the fullest.

"If an egg is broken by an outside force, life ends but if an egg is broken by an inside force, life begins. Great things always begin from the inside." (Demp, 2014)

Discovery means that something is hidden and must be exposed. In most cases, when we refer to a hidden substance, people generally assume that we must be talking of treasures (i.e. hidden treasures) and such hidden treasures are expensive, which could comprise of many resources such as gold, silver, copper, diamonds and steel. These resources are scarce because of their value, and it may take hard work to dig them out of their hidden places even after their discovery.

Self-discovery is quite similar to this kind of activity because you have to put a lot of hard work into discovering your true self-identity; and, after that, you have to manage that identity so that it can fully deliver its value to humanity and fulfil its maximum potential.

The characteristics discussed here are meant to make an individual more specific in relation to his or her identify. People need to ask those questions that will generate innovative conclusions of the kind of person that they've always been and the kind of person that they are actually meant to be.

PROCESSES AND STAGES OF SIM DEVELOPMENT.

STAGE 1:

Planning yourself - Planning means that you have seen ahead and you need to know the steps to take before you can achieve what you can see in the future. So, you must strategize yourself to fulfil what you've envisioned for the future. These steps entail proper planning and unless you build a plan around anything and everything that you do, it is practically impossible that you will achieve anything. For instance, you have decided to go somewhere to meet a friend the next day. Somebody who values himself or herself would be expected to plan this meeting: awakening early to get dressed and to leave the house in order to get to the venue on time.

We all have plans, but our problems are that we only create the plans in our minds or with our lips – we are not ready to commit to these plans.

If you're not ready to discipline yourself to work according to your plans then planning becomes as useless as not planning. As you might have known, planning is the first stage of every idea/work/project/business. If you can get the planning right from the onset and you're ready to commit yourself to executing the plans, it is possible that you will eventually succeed in implementing those plans and get the results that you've envisaged or something quite similar to the result that you've projected.

STAGE 2:

Doing it yourself - For every action there must be a reaction. Something must be done to activate something that can make us fully achieve our goals and that action must be managed properly. As stated in the explanation for planning, it is essential that we put all our concentration and quality time into any plan that we decide to make. It is easier to think of ideas than it is to plan a strategy and it is more difficult to commit to executing that strategy, which is an act of doing it yourself. The process of executing an idea is proportional to the energy that has been committed to planning and the willingness to making use of the resources that have been identified in the plan as the requirements for fulfilling the idea. There is an expected end or result for every action.

Before you commit to doing anything, you must have a clear aim or objective for doing it and that is why it's necessary to envisage an end result for whatever actions you are taking. This can be very helpful if you can picture the end result of your actions from the beginning (i.e. during the planning stage)

STAGE 3:

Monitoring yourself - In order for you to monitor yourself, we have a few metrics that need to be considered and one of these is the Self-Performance Indicator (SPI); this determines how far you've gone in achieving what you set to achieve for yourself.

Without metrics, there is no measurement because measurement is the result of monitoring something or someone against a variable. There is always a process to everything, even if that process is a minor task; there is a good way of doing something and there are better ways of doing the same thing, while we also have the best way of executing the same task. People often actually give up looking for the best way of doing things when they've found a better way to execute a task;

however, they make it sound as if that is actually the best way to do the same task.

In doing just anything, we would have to monitor the process of executing the plans; and, in monitoring the actions taken we would need to have our eyes fixed on what it is that we are expecting to see as an end result; hence we might be tempted to think that we have achieved something when, in fact, we have not even got anywhere close to the end result. Processes are there to guide us in making the best decision – not to resolve to or adhere to any suggestion that comes to mind. Individually speaking, we are supposed to have our own processes for executing any plans that we have. We shouldn't conclude that whatever plans that worked for the other person will definitely work for us; as people are different in so many ways, those plans might not work exactly for us as they did for the other person. Monitoring oneself involves searching for ways that worked, as well as endeavouring to configure a special platform or set of processes that can be adapted to different aspects of one's life. One should have a process in place on how to deal with success, failures, emotions, love, joy, excitement and pain. The ways that we deal with these entities are individually different and we shouldn't judge people who are dealing with these things differently as if they're weird or abnormal. It is through the process of monitoring that we begin to realize that certain things we accomplish naturally are very different from how others fulfil similar tasks.

STAGE 4:

Controlling yourself - Standards, rules, obligations and disciplines must be in place for Self Identification Management (SIM).

You measure your achievements against the standards you've set for yourself, that is, you set the rules and then control yourself against the rules set through self-discipline. The moment that you decide to do something and you begin to plan for it; this simply means that you want to control how these things are taken care of and how the plan will be implemented.

If plans can control almost every decision, then it's right for us to say that, if we can plan most of our actions (we cannot plan all actions, even if we try), then it is possible for us to have more control over how these plans are executed and to have control over the outcome of our actions. We create the control that we want when we create a plan, and while executing the plan we also exercise another form of control over its execution and its end result if it meets our expectation or if there is need for an adjustment.

Controlling yourself to be better means that there are areas in your life that you want to improve. It is then, that you set targets that you want to meet and, by doing this, you put a control over yourself not to go beyond the target that you've set for yourself.

Every individual should endeavour to do this more often as it takes them from their present stage in life to the next stage, where they can advance and achieve more in life.

STAGE 5:

Maintaining yourself - Maintaining the previous steps can lead to full achievement of Self Identification Management. All the processes of SIM are iterative and may be used at any time in the process of managing self-identify; hence, a standard should be available for maintaining yourself. Maintenance occurs as a result of an existing process or plan.

When we talk of maintenance, we are simply saying that we don't want these things to go down in value or worth, so we need to do everything possible to make them stay as they are or even get better, if possible.

As a person, you cannot maintain yourself unless you've identified who you are – that is why I believe that it is very important that anybody reading this book must be willing to identify themselves. When you have finished reading this book and you've identified who you are, then you can start maintaining what you've identified as your key strengths, values, assets, capabilities and worth. These are some of the things that would make people believe that you are who you say you are to them, through your identity. The price you pay for maintenance is not as expensive as the price you pay when you're just beginning to develop or manufacture the same product: what matters most is that there is a maintenance measure that has been put in place to prevent the product from decaying or losing value.

In order that we have a better understanding of how important it is for us to maintain ourselves, I decided to paint the picture of a product losing its value when it doesn't undergo maintenance; in as much as we are trying to be successful (assuming that everyone wants to be successful in whatever they do). The SIM model is for us to identify ourselves with and begin to use as a means of becoming successful so that we can give something back.

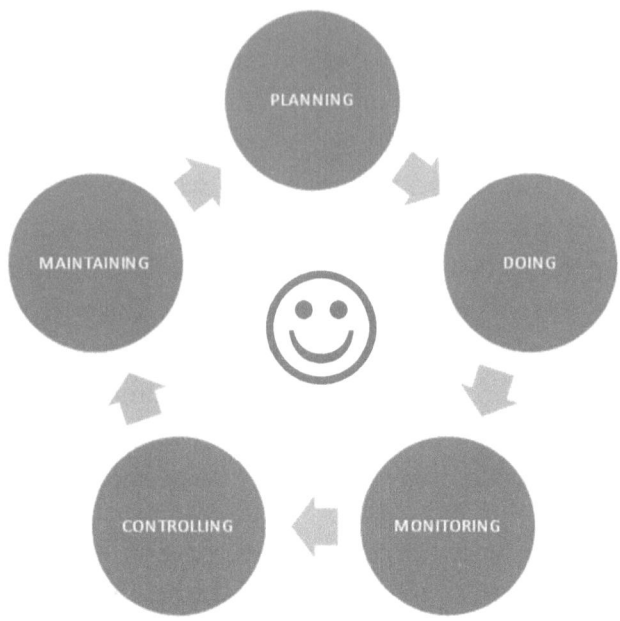

<u>Diagram showing the processes and stages for SIM Development.</u>

Principles of SIM

In order for SIM processes to be fully adhered to, they must possess these principles as follows:

- They must be desirable
- They must be measurable
- They must be result and goal-oriented
- They must be achievable

SELF-IDENTIFICATION PLAN (SIP)

In as much as there are many plans available for different reasons and different functions, so also must there be a plan for you to achieve your SIM, which is what we are discussing in this manual. Various aspects of life and businesses are concerned with a multiplicity of plans, such as business plans, stage plans, strategy plans, project plans, development plans, action plans, business development plans, health development plans, and service plans.

These plans are made available for certain reasons; principally, to propose what is about to happen in the execution of a task: how to do it, who should do it, why it should be done and the benefits of doing it. A plan is also meant to list the things that may be necessary for the achievement of any task or project to be implemented or developed. Therefore, in order to fully understand the management of your identity, you need to put some kind of plan into place and strictly monitor its progress and control. The saying "A fool at 40 is a fool forever" implies that a person who does not understand the management of his or her identify by a certain age is not fit to be called a mature person, because a person will surely be discerned by their identity and this can only be achieved by managing self-identity. In the same way that a person is identified as a mature person before he or she reaches 40, so also it is illegal for children below the age of 18 to do certain things, which are against the law; hence the under 18s have to show their ID cards so that public attendants can confirm that they are in fact of that age.

TYPES OF SELF-IDENTIFICATION MANAGEMENT

Custom/Patterned SIM: This kind of SIM theory is based on the experience of others or written experience of people who have been involved with SIM and have therefore realized their self-actualization (Maslow, 1987). Therefore, this becomes apparent for others to follow these people's patterned way of living as a habit that can help others to experience a life of self-fulfilment.

Tailored SIM: An experience that is specially suited for that purpose and at that time. This type of SIM is supported by determination and dedicated to the kind of lifestyle that is best suited to personal self-actualization. Tailored SIM is designed and managed in such a way that it fulfils a particular purpose or intention in which it has been designed. It is akin to a bespoke lifestyle that is specially made or manufactured for that person alone and can only be achieved through rigorous understanding of that first step towards self-actualization, which is *self-identification* and is a preliminary to managing the process of actualization. It is a specific and appropriate design that must be adapted in order for self-actualization to be realized.

Trendy or existing SIM: This theory is based on the recent practices that are in vogue as regards the way to manage identification of self. It simply means that you are recognizing your gifts, talents or strengths because of what you see the celebrities do on TV or from the common practices of your peers. (For instance, tattoos are now in vogue because David Beckham and other stars and celebrities flaunt these; likewise, many people are beginning to recognize their football skills because they see for themselves what Lionel Messi, a world's best player, is doing on the football pitch.)

LAWS OF SELF IDENTIFICATION MANAGEMENT

These five laws encompass SIM practises directed towards the fulfilment of goals with passion.

Law of Reflection: This law states that *"Your true self will be revealed to you when a self-examination is carried out and reported back to you."* The act of pondering on previous actions or reactions, whether good or bad, impacts on the present in relation to the lessons learnt. It's also called the meditation law of SIM. Reflection is the same as if you are staring at a mirror to see your beauty and for the mirror to reveal who in fact you are. It is another way of understanding what constitutes your being. When a light reflects in your face, it is not the actual light that you are seeing but a resemblance of the light, which may be assumed to be the actual light.

Reflection in a human being happens when one gives himself or herself a thorough examination or check-up; in the process, this reveals who you are or who you've portrayed yourself to represent in front of others around you or those you've encountered. Reflection is not meant to discourage you; it is meant to report back to you how you've presented yourself to people.

Law of Endurance: This law states that *"the one who is wise enough to start a race is not as wise as the one who finishes the race."* Starting a race is a temporary commitment, but finishing the race is a deep commitment for achievement, which requires a huge amount of endurance.

The act of endurance for greatness is the act of preparing for hardship because greatness comes from hardship or challenges. There can never be any form of greatness without hardship or challenges and there is no challenge without an exit point from such experiences. The ability to quickly identify the exit point from hardship is what differentiates the great from the ordinary. During this endurance process, there's a period of waiting and preparation for the manifestation of your full potential; however, it is only with determination and persistence that you will be able to move ahead of these challenges to actualize your goals.

Law of Continuity: This law states that *"you must continue to increase your knowledge and passion for becoming great."* Increase comes when the passion to achieve is greater than the fear of failure. The increase might not be visible at first; however, through commitment and persistence, it will be obvious for all to see and appreciate your effort. People will not buy into your idea; they will buy into the passion for your responsibility and your diligence to become great.

The skill of continuity in the pursuit of success is the greatest skill of all. Great achievement comes neither easily nor cheaply; therefore, one must be willing to try anything and everything to acquire success – which can only happen through the continual effort of doing something to achieve the goal.

Law of Connectivity: This law states that *"the gap between your desired goal and your present accomplishment requires a thorough understanding of your ability to continue a process that leads to your success."* Connectivity involves two points or junctions that need to be connected together and this means that someone or something must replace the gap in between those two points or find a way to complement the gap. Understanding what should replace or fill the gap between those two points gives a clearer view of how to cross over to the other side (i.e. desired goal). In order to achieve greatness or add value to themselves, only those who have identified themselves will be able to use their visions to connect with others and connect others to their visions. Longevity is not connectivity, but connectivity depends solely on how well you're able to relate cordially with people of diverse interests or with various perspectives (i.e. not how far but how well). The more you can connect with likeminded people, the easier it is for them to carry your vision and bring you closer to achieving your goals than you would have done single-handedly. Our level of connectivity can be limited for reasons that are beyond our capacity; we can, however, create a platform or atmosphere in order to have an unlimited channel of connecting with our goals or purpose in life.

Access to connecting with your future may be hindered by features that are beyond your control; this may only be a temporary hindrance for your comeback, but you have to be willing to unravel additional access that will eventually take you to that desired goal with no more limitations. *"Vision creates a sight for us but our minds connect us to the object."*

Law of Alignment: This law states that *"there is a fixed path for everyone to achieve individual success but aligning with your individual path of success takes deep understanding of who you are and what you're placed here on earth to achieve."* There is nothing as important as the alignment of vision with passion, which invariably brings about fulfilment of purpose. A person who is aligned to his/her vision is already half-fulfilled.

Law of Identity: This law states that *"my identity is a reflection of who I am and this is determined by how much understanding that I have about myself."* A man or woman who understands himself or herself must have a thorough and absolute understanding of themselves and this doesn't mean that they only know their names and where they live.

It involves identifying why they have been called that name, what the name represents, where they live and why they act like they do.

If you understand the concept of this law at any early stage of your life, it will be very possible for you to use it to your own advantage rather than allowing people to use it to your disadvantage. This law is an additional rule in support of all other information presented in this book towards identifying one's self.

Law of Commitment

The law of commitment states that *"whatever you are committed to do will be committed to you, which means that commitment is reciprocal."*

SIM ANALYSIS (SA)

Self Identification Management analysis is a broad study of how to manage self-identity. The study uncovers some vital facts and you must act on them with the intention of turning the awkward ones to your own advantage, so that they serve as your strengths and not your weaknesses. In the process of SIM analysis, you have to set some questions that your analysis will have to answer, so that you can measure the importance of analyzing who you are and what is your unique purpose here on earth.

If you feel that you're living according to your purpose of creation and are satisfied with what you've achieved so far and do not want to go further than where you are, then you may not need to analyse yourself. Maybe faith or luck have meant that you are satisfied with the state that you are in, but I can tell you that there are better offers and opportunities out there if only you can specifically analyse yourself to tap into some of them. This is why we've always been told to think in an original or different manner; hence, we should think beyond our comfort zones and seek more opportunities outside our normal routines.

In order to successfully participate in this analysis of SIM, you must first analyse the trends in your past successes, disappointments and failures that have led you to where you are and the position you occupy now; then you can easily project yourself to where you might want to be. These trends also represent future opportunities and strategies that may help in the decision-making steps to be taken and the risks to get involved in.

During SIM analysis you can identify the trend in your unconscious or conscious efforts that can lead to success or failure. You then understand how your body system reacts to certain actions or responsibilities, which can either take you higher or displace you from your goal set; this will in turn determine what you should focus your strengths on. When you do analyse yourself, you prepare yourself to make some changes that will later affect you positively; in order not to regret taking such steps, you must do these tasks with great care. Because of this analysis, it is therefore necessary that you strictly follow your SIP (*Self-Identification Plan*), which must direct you towards the scope of achieving your set goals.

SIM should not in any way be classified as 'egocentric' or 'egoism'. 'Ego' is only focusing on the importance of yourself over others, but if you truly know yourself and you have identified who you truly are, then you should know that you cannot be egocentric and still be successful because people are there to support you or engage in your quest for success, otherwise you will only be avoiding the issue. As it's been mentioned earlier, you cannot be identified by others if you have not studied yourself enough to know who you really are and what constitutes the real you. You must, therefore, focus not only on yourself but also on identifying yourself and how to manage your self-identity, so that others can identify you with the way you've identified yourself, such as the way you talk, walk and do virtually everything. It is on the basis of this self-identification that others will value you, because you have already taken time to rigorously find your self-identity and they now have to accept and value the identity you've given to yourself.

It would be difficult to cast your vote for a leader who cannot describe his or her vision for the post they are contesting. It is a situation akin to where the leader does not fully understand himself or herself;

furthermore, how would he or she know the identity of his followers. If you have truly and sincerely identified yourself, then you would have the authority in your own territory to become a monopoly in your area of expertise.

We all have our own different weaknesses or something that makes us frightened, but it is only the truly bold, strong individuals who seek help when they are really weak in certain circumstances. Therefore, we have to identify with that point where we can easily tell when to seek help and know exactly what kind of help we seek and where to get it.

You are not only strong because you have no weaknesses, but you are stronger when you know your weaknesses. Furthermore, you're willing to prevent these from discouraging you from moving forwards to achieve that set goal; on the other hand, you work so hard on them in order to benefit from the weaknesses and they now create opportunities for you instead.

In order to analyse your self-identity, you can simply answer these four questions that clearly lay out your SIM analysis:

1. What do I have that others don't have? (Strength)
2. What do they have that I don't have? (Weakness)
3. How do I use what I have? (Opportunity)
4. Where can I get what I don't have? (Threat)

What do I have that others don't have?	What do they have that I don't have?
How do I use what I have?	Where can I get what I don't have?

Illustration table for SIM analysis

This table illustrates the importance of SIM analysis in identifying your true self: you can use these questions to discover your uniqueness and what you need to do to fulfil destiny. Many people go about doing whatever they can find, not considering whether it goes with their core value or if it will help them to fulfil their purpose. When you can identify what you possess that many other people do not have, you stand the chance to create a niche for yourself by making use of that opportunity (i.e. filling the gap) and this will certainly increase your self-confidence. You can also consider the statement at the right of the table, which proposes a question about what other people have, but you don't. This shows that although you have some things that others don't have, you also lack some things that others have. How do you gain those things that others have but you don't have? And, how then do you manage the strengths, skills or talents that you have but others don't have? These are some critical questions for us and only a practise such as SIM analysis can reveal the answers to us.

RESOURCES OF SIM

During SIM analysis we must consider the resources that will be required for us to complete and achieve our SIM. Listed below are some of the resources that are needed, so as for us to fully comprehend both our uniqueness and self-identity:

> *Internal resources*: such as mind, intuition, motivation, spirit, energy, willingness, conviction, and confidence.

> *External resources*: such as skills, talents, networking, experiences, and team working.

> *Self-Modelling:* Self-modelling is a way of identifying the standards and requirements that can propel a person straight from where they are to where they want to be. This could be where they dream of getting to or what they've visualized of achieving as a person. To self-model, one has to investigate oneself inwardly, consider the views of other people and analyse all relevant findings before evaluating any option, or reaching any conclusions about self-identification. While this is being done, one has to define the pattern of achieving those things identified as part of the self-identity or the change that one needs to implement in order to complete SIM. It should be noted that SIM cannot be effective without properly considering the steps of self-modelling, self-performance indicator (SPI), and critical self-success factor (CSSF).

Critical Self-Success Factor (CSSF): Critical Self-Success Factors are those little things that might not mean so much to you but they do determine a lot about the successes that you've achieved in the past and those that you're yet to achieve; with less or no struggle at all. Because we have identified these things mean that we are likely to succeed, provided that we continue doing what we know how to do best and monitor that our CSSFs are still intact, so as to complete SIM.

FACTORS FOR SIM ANALYSIS

There are certain factors that can prevent us from duly obliging to our SIM practices and I can only mention five of them in this book:

i. Time
ii. Passion
iii. Character
iv. Attitude
v. Communication

Time: The essence of managing self is that we are time-bound and the earlier we realize that we are growing older by the second and not by the year, as many of us would have thought, the better. Every second that passes proves that we are a little older than we were a few minutes earlier; therefore, we ought to be aware of that fact and act consciously. When on this planet Earth, all of us make deadlines for the activities that we engage in; we would individually return to where we came from, but the time spent on earth should be used wisely, which is why we are advocating that people should quickly identify their self at an early stage, so that they can begin to manage it for full satisfaction and fulfilment. There is always a time to achieve certain goals and if that time goes by, it may be very difficult to find an opportunity that will allow such gifts or talents to be accomplished.

For example, you may have always had a passion to play football when you were younger but were deprived of the opportunity to play. Some years later, you abandoned that ambition and got on with doing something else that didn't give you pleasure but at least it's able to allow you pay your bills and sort your life out for the time being. The football gift became outdated after a certain age because of old age (let's say 50) and no one expected you to utilize that gift anymore – it became dormant in you, which was extremely painful and disheartening. This is one of the many reasons why we should endeavour to identify our gifts or talents at an early stage, so that we can begin to work on them by developing them more until we become experts in such fields.

In an encounter I had with using time poorly, I learnt much about time well-spent. I was in the middle of writing an article on mind exploration and I was feeling so excited because of the inspirations that I was receiving, even before I started composing the article and writing it down. I didn't want to be distracted and I was getting really fascinated by the article. Then I received a call from one of my business partners who wanted to give me feedback regarding an option that we were working on and that was based on his findings. However, instead of ignoring the call, I decided to take it. Before I did that, I had just thought of a great idea for the article that I was composing, but I didn't have enough time to quickly take a note of this idea before the call. Because I had calculated that I was going to talk for only a few seconds before telling him to call me back, and not knowing that the conversation would be interesting to me, I had forgotten that I was doing something else before the call.

It was after having a conversation with him for more than five minutes that I realized I was thinking of a great idea that could have made the article both interesting and exciting to read. It was then I had thoughts about that one second when I should have switched the phone off or told him to ring me back when I had finished composing the article. I can still remember how fantastic the idea or ideas might have been had I not been interrupted.

We should not forget that the Sun and the Moon value time more than anything and that is why we can hardly see them overlapping one another. Both celestial bodies know their time and they come out when they have to and go back in at the right time. This is a very critical example that shows the power of SIM: the Sun and the Moon have identified their own times of brightness and they stick to these times without any interference from other parties and that is why they can never be overlooked because they can manage their own identities. The Sun rises due east and sets due west, while the Moon comes and goes at the appropriate time. It is as simple as that, but it could be more complicated if neither of them was unable to manage *self-identification*.

These are some of the statements that you would naturally make when you think of time as a factor of SIM:

- Is it time for me to do it?
- Can it wait till tomorrow?
- The last time I did it was last year.
- It's been long since I did it; when next can I do it?
- I will do it next year when I'm fully ready to do it.
- I don't think I have the time to do it now.

These statements are some of the many excuses that we constantly give or say to ourselves to help us prevent time from taking its real course; besides, we are not conscious that when we say that we are saving time, we are actually wasting time, and as a consequence, we are wasting ourselves and our lives in general. Time is static and cannot be moved forwards or backwards. We have the power, however, to run faster or do things faster and we have the option of doing them slowly, depending on what we choose to do.

45

Passion: Nothing can be achieved without passion and the importance of this emotion cannot be overemphasized. Whatever a person does, he or she must do it with passion before they can achieve any success; this is not only because passion breeds energy and anxiety as passion moves people to do things even when they don't feel like exerting themselves.

Passion is more like a driver who drives you to do what you ought to be doing; it also identifies what you should be doing and doesn't let you rest until you finally get back to doing it. Passion is powerful and should be handled with care and determination. It is closely related and affected by your emotions because you tend to have more feelings for things that are borne out of passion. There's this feeling that you get when something good is happening to you or when great things are about to happen to you. If you can perceive success from afar, it means that you can feel it coming closer to you than you could imagine, and this will indirectly affect your emotions in a positive way. If you know this, whatever you desire or have interest in will make you begin to build up some emotions around it and invariably you will want to know and hear more about it. Your emotions direct all other parts of you and channel those parts to your passion, especially when it comes to decision-making.

We make some critical decisions based on how we are feeling at that point, even when we try to prevent our emotions from being revealed. Taking risks is catalysed by a greater level of our emotions because we have to selectively choose one option out of many, and this would mean that we either choose the right option or the wrong one; however, we wouldn't know which is the right one or the wrong one until we've made our selection. We have positive emotions which are categorized as love, care, like, good, splendid, awesome, gorgeous, glamorous, beauty, and so on; while the following are negative types of emotions: hatred, jealousy, envy and dislike.

Passion provides the reasons to make statements like these:

- I think I'm better off doing that one than doing this one
- I am not meant to be in this situation
- I think I will just quit this job and go with my passion
- I might just suffocate if I'm not given the chance to sing
- I don't think I'm meant to work for someone else but myself
- This is not what I enjoy doing
- Although I don't get paid, I will keep on doing this

These are some of the likely statements that keep ringing in the ears of someone with passion for something other than what they are engaged in right now; such statements make people feel so uncomfortable, wherever they might be until they actually get to where they are meant to be. Where your passion is, you tend to make time for it. Passion, as a factor of SIM analysis can be simplified by going through the principles of SIM, as highlighted in an earlier page of this book.

I would like to describe the proposition that I presented during an event "Harnessing Passion" and mention three principles for harnessing passion in us:

1. **Preparation**: *Passion will not take you anywhere unless you're prepared for it.*

2. **Purpose:** *For your passion to be realized there must be a purpose.*

3. **Profit**: *Profit drives passion and vice versa.*

Character: Human beings possess individual characters that distinguish them from other people, even if they come from the same family or grow up in the same background. The quality of someone's personality can easily be identified by their character and it shows the nature of what they possess in their innermost being. People tend to display some of the traits of what they have been exposed to rather than feeling of what they think is right. Our characters define us to people whom we are meeting for the first time; people can easily use such information to describe us to others, based on what they've encountered in getting to know us for the first time, that is, it's very scary not to manage our self-identity through the characters that we display to others.

Formerly, after a two-hour conversation with people I had met, I would have been able to relate a few things that I had observed about those people within the short period of time that I had spent with them.

This manifests how quickly your character can speak; and, you should take time to listen to your characters because they are reminding you whether they want you to change or maintain that particular character you possess.

Here are some statements that can help us to understand what character does to our SIM:

- I think I speak fluently all the time
- He deals kindly to everyone
- It's so funny that she doesn't even know that she snubs everyone
- When will you stand up to your responsibilities?

Statements like these imply that someone's character is being mentioned or analysed, and people are seriously taking note of certain points of character in order to understand an individual.

Attitude: Whether positive or negative, attitude in itself is the barrier-breaker (ice-breaker) because it breaks the barrier between what our minds are thinking and what we later decide to do. Whether we behave badly or good, it is not because we are generally bad or we are surprisingly good; it is because of our attitude towards that person or thing and that is why we may decide to either be good or bad, except for circumstances beyond our imagination, which can sometimes affect our outward delivery. The best way to work around circumstances even when they try to knock us down is by creating a fence-like positive attitude that we can use to counter the effect of having a negative attitude. The moment the negative thought tries to creep into the subconscious mind, the fence-like positive attitude prevents it and it bounces back out because it's not permitted to penetrate into the conscious mind.

The following statements describe certain attitudes to SIM analysis:

- Whether it rains or not, I must attend the conference
- I don't see any reason why I shouldn't make the phone call, even if he's not going to answer the phone
- We shall see that the field is greener on the other side when we get there
- Without any doubt we have to win the world cup

The following quote is one of the many quotes that I've scooped out of my articles and I feel it describes what attitude actually means. *"Attitude is an internal force that produces a positive or negative outward expression."* ~ Temitayo Oyediran

Communication: I believe that there are two sets of people involved with communication: the *speaker* and the *listener*. The reason why communication is one of the factors that affects SIM analysis is because we have to communicate who we are to other people – people who are running our vision or those who are striving to fulfil a particular purpose in life. *"People are your great asset"* and *"people are the most difficult creature to deal with"*, I have learnt a great deal from these two phrases and I don't think I can easily forget the lessons learnt from them. Let me quickly explain the lessons learnt from these phrases.

I learnt that when you have the right people around you, then you are blessed to have them because they will make life easier for you;

otherwise, they may make life miserable for you if they are not managed properly. The second phrase is simply saying that people generally are very difficult to deal with unless you learn how to manage them in order to get the best out of them. How then do you manage people around you so that you can get the best out of them?

Communicating with people goes beyond having a conversation, which must be mutual, where the speaker and listener are benefitting from the conversation. Communication not only involves talking but also listening in order to gain thorough understanding of the discussion. How do you communicate your identity to people who are ready to buy into your vision or idea if you cannot manage your own self-identify? How would people follow you or make you a role model in order to achieve any goal if they realize that you truly do not even know yourself? This attitude is akin to the confusion expressed in the idiom "the blind leading the blind". Everything in this life revolves round leadership because either you are leading people towards yourself or you are leading them away from you; and, you may be leading yourself to more opportunities or taking yourself far away from them. Communicating with people in various ways portray your leadership style – it is a choice that one must take whether they like it or not. These are some statements to show that effective communication can boost your SIM.

- Acting out what you intend to say to those who matter in a situation

- Displaying what you plan to say or indicate about an illustration or rich picture

- Presenting a map-out route or path for executing a goal

- Painting a bigger picture of what you hope to achieve as part of your vision

Before trying to communicate with people about our missions and visions, there are many ways that we can communicate to them about how we have taken the time to engage SIM practices.

According to Priestley (2010) in: *Become a Key Person of Influence (KPI): 5 step sequence to becoming one of the most highly valued and highly paid people in your industry*, a key person of influence is someone who must be vital and not functional. Vital people are key to any industry: they are the key people of influence and are irreplaceable, but functional people can be easily replaced.

Every KPI needs to have an 'Eiffel Tower – something impressive and unique that others can talk about with their friends (i.e. micro-niche is your Eiffel Tower)'. (p. 28) According to Priestley we all have something within us that we need to give for people to recognize us as the KPI in that industry. *"You are already standing on a mountain of value. Your story is valuable, your experience is unique, and you are worth your weight in gold... just as you are."* (pp. 48–49)

Basically, what Daniel Priestley was saying in the quote above is that we need to identify our uniqueness before we can become a Key Person of Influence, so that people will see us as vital in our industries or whatever we do. This is what Self –Identification Management encourages when we implement its practices.

GROW WITH SIM

Ageing is just for you but growing is about yourself and for the benefit of others.

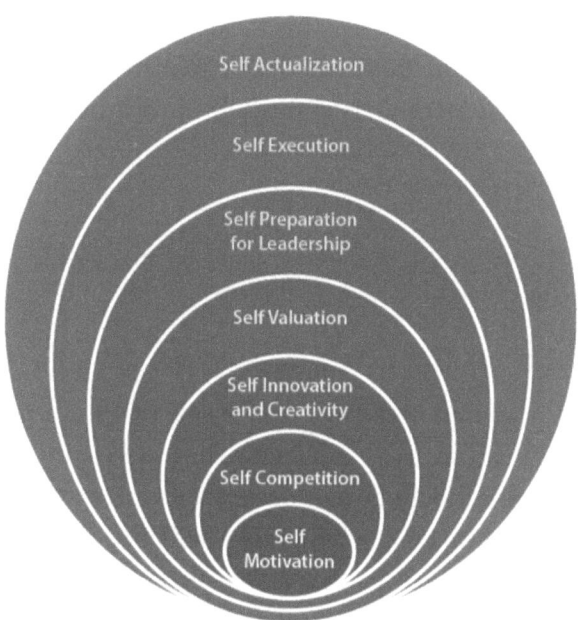

Methods on how to grow with SIM

Self-motivation

Firstly, what is self-motivation?

Self-motivation is not the art of doing something. It is defined as the means by which you inspire or encourage yourself to do what needs to be done.

I wrote an article about motivation, which I have found to be very illustrative as regards this topic on self-motivation and I will quickly analyse it in order to explain the phenomenon.

Self-motivation can be very effective when we are conscious of three things which are internal to us. This means that we can easily control these things if we wish, or we can decide to disregard them and then they will control us by rendering our self-motivation dormant.

Three keys to effective self-motivation

- Mind
- Mission
- Move

Everyone is composed of a mind and inside of this mind are issues that can affect a person. We should take time to identify such entities, or even better, the thoughts that occupy our minds and then begin to manage them properly, so that they will not take us where we don't want to go. A person's mind is like a controller that guides and directs their motives and actions; therefore, the mind has the power to control someone to do what he or she doesn't want to do. This is a simple explanation of the importance of the mind and we should take good care of it, so that it will favour us rather than disfavour us. For instance, a car has many parts, but the steering wheel is a vital part of any vehicle that controls the direction in which the vehicle goes. The vehicle only goes where the steering wheel directs it to go and it is the same with our minds. A person is directed by his or her mind and we tend to go where our minds direct us to go; this is why it is important to consider the thoughts that come out of the mind and manage them effectively, because these thoughts can be the determining factors of any decision to be taken by the carrier or possessor of the mind.

When a mind is to make any decision, certain things have to be considered and one of them is the mission behind a proposal. When a thought comes to mind, it comes because of a reason and that reason must have a positive effect on the personality of the carrier or possessor. I believe the reason for taking that decision can motivate the person to take the decision or not and that is why it's an act of self-motivation.

Similarly, when a decision is made internally and all other parts of the body have agreed to comply with the same decision, the next thing to do is to make a move in relation to the decision – acting on the decision that has been chosen. The move that we are talking about here is the action on the outside, which is externally displayed to people, although the process started from inside (i.e. the mind). The self-motivated human being is someone who exercises his or her mind to think extensively on the situation in hand and who then engages on a mission for their choice of action.

Therefore, self-motivation makes someone do things based on internal decisions or convictions and not on external influences.

I can draw a few points from my article on *'Motivation'*, even though we are talking of self-motivation:

> In order for the *'Motivator'* to inspire the *'Motivatee'* (i.e. a person to be motivated), there must be a reason behind the action and that is what I call **MISSION**. People don't just respond to changes but they need to be given the

reasons to do so and that is why both the *'Motivator'* and *'Motivatee'* need to be highly motivated, in order to achieve a successful level of motivation. (Oyediran, 2013)

In line with self-motivation, the above text connotes that the motivator and the person to be motivated should both exercise self-motivation practices but in the case of SIM; both the motivator and the motivatee can be one person.

> It is the mind that enhances motivation, which drives every other part of the body. I will say, a motivated mind is a motivated body. If you are motivated from the inside, it will quickly and obviously reflect on the outside. While many people are focusing on the effects of motivation to be seen on the outside, it would have to complete the process of inner motivation. The difference between inner motivation and outer motivation is that one is temporary while the other one could be permanent, if maintained and controlled properly. If the mind of an individual is motivated towards success, even if the success does not come as early as possible; the drive to succeed will keep pushing him until it comes but if the person is only motivated on the outside, the **MIND** (inner motivation) is not strong enough to handle the waiting, so it will break down and give up (i.e. temporary motivation).

> It is possible to be the *'Motivator'* and the *'Motivatee'*, if one can easily motivate himself/herself to have a change of mind that will move for change. (Oyediran, 2013)

This extract from the article on motivation emphasizes that self-motivation engages the mind to control other parts of the human body, and if motivated on the inside, it will be adequately reflected on the outside.

Action plan for self-motivation

The following steps may help to enhance your level of motivation:

Step 1: Understand that you can do more than you are presently doing.

Step 2: Identify those things that are limiting factors to you and deal with them.

Step 3: Try to find a way to reduce or eliminate those limiting factors inside you.

Step 4: Push yourself to do those things that seem difficult for you to do.

Step 5: If you still can't do those things, try again many times before you ask for help.

Step 6: Don't just get help but learn from it so that you won't need it again.

Step 7: Aim mainly at those things that look big and complicated to you, and then use them to sharpen your skills.

Step 8: Press forwards; you've progressed a long way ahead than to turn back now.

Self-competition

When we talk of competition, we immediately think of two or more people competing against each other. Competition, however, can also be within one person and that is the essence of this manual.

Before I go any further, I will like to ask this question:

What is competition? The dictionary describes competition as an act that involves two or more objects in order to gain a profit or get a reward for being outstanding.

In as much as I would like to agree with this definition, I want to add that competition may also be practised by one person alone, which is what I call self-competition.

Let me briefly explain...

I describe competition as a way whereby to set a goal and strive to achieve it, but this can be done by one person or by many people at the same time.

If you set a goal to be better than you were yesterday, you have no choice other than to *compete* with yourself or additional factors, such as laziness, food, friends, discouraging words and other limiting factors that may set in and prevent you from achieving that goal. When your mind has been set to achieve a goal, you should place your trust in those who can help you to achieve it, although the competition is still for you and *you* alone.

In most cases, people tend to think of competition as a way whereby they stay ahead of others or where they are competing with others to win a race; in its actual sense, competition goes further and it should be seen as an inward decision for a person or a business to be competitive with previous successes.

Let me explain further...

For instance, an athlete may be competing with other athletes who are preparing for the same race. I believe that, most of the time, the athlete who practises and prepares more will eventually win the race, while the others will come behind. But what if all the athletes decide not to practise at all because they feel that others wouldn't practise as well? Alternatively, they may merely be lazy and not put real effort into winning the race. Then it becomes obvious that the level of competition is determined by the level of preparation of all the competitors or athletes.

If, however, you're simply competing with yourself, based on your previous best achievements, then it becomes irrelevant whether someone else (i.e. your competitor or another athlete) is practising or not.

Therefore, it is imperative that we all look inwardly and try to compete with only our previous successes and achievements rather than looking elsewhere for competitors or people to compete with.

In whatever you do, you must have previously achieved something, and your focus should be on how to do things better on a daily basis; at the end of a year, you could then look back and realize that you've actually been stretching yourself to become better. Your previous achievements should not be your *finishing line* – they should be your *starting point* for greater things – because that is where your own personal competition starts from. Where your *goals* are concerned, you should make your first great achievement your guideline for other future achievements and ensure that you don't go below the Achievement Standard that you've set for yourself. This strategy will also benefit you to develop a KPI (i.e. metric), which can help you understand, when you're not acceding to your Achievement Standard.

The process of analysing self-competition must be based on your Achievement Standard. If the prize or reward ascribes to any competition is below your standard, then it is not the best option for you and should not be given any priority.

"Competing with others is a contest but competing with yourself is a complement of yourself." (Oyediran, 2014)

Diagram showing a Self-competitive athlete.

Competitive analysis can be described as a review and analysis of all our competitions (both inward and outward), whether they relate to past, present or future competitions.

There are two types of competition:

1) Inward competition: (i.e. competition with self and within.)
2) Outward competition: (i.e. competition with others and without.)

There's always a motive behind every competition and the reason must be genuine enough for you to embark on the journey of self-competition or competing with other people.

In all our competitions, we must ensure that our past achievements do not surpass our present ones, while the present achievements do not surpass the future ones. This is what is called *growing up steadily.*

This discussion on self-competition may be associated with one of Abraham Lincoln's numerous quotes:

"I don't think much of a man who is not wiser today than he was yesterday."

(Krieger, 2002)

In other words, self-competition is the continuous growth or improvement of one's self by ourselves in order to achieve more today than what we've already achieved before.

I never knew how competitive I was until I actually thought of my actions back in my university days. It was then that I pondered on the best way possible for me to compete with the so-called 'rich kids' in my university; being a private school (glorified secondary school) you get to see children of influential people in the country, residing in the same hostel with you and you hear them talking about how they travel in and out of the UK and America, just to go and enjoy their summer holidays there. I was the child of the typical man with two or three children, whose main interest was to see that his children had the best education and not a flashy lifestyle, even though he had the money to give them that kind of lifestyle. I was not just an ordinary child; I was exceptional because I've always loved to stand out, if not in anything else but definitely in the way I dressed. Because I couldn't impress my fellow students with my proposed sophisticated dressing, and anyway those rich kids could have bought even more expensive and finer clothes than I could afford, I had no way of competing with them. However, I thought of this idea of waiting till the middle of the semester when most people (those who travelled abroad and those who did not) had finished showing off their new clothes; it was then that I planned my trip to the most up-to-date boutiques in Lagos, Nigeria to buy the latest but scarce designer clothes at that time and that no one had bought. Then I would be the first person to wear it in my school. This plan helped me to gain some attention for myself, although I did not come from a rich family, but people thought we were well off because of the way I came across to them with my designer clothes. I applied the same principle to my education, whereby I thought that even if I'm not the best in dressing, nor the best in partying or playing basketball, then why couldn't I work on myself so that at least I could become one of the best in my class or maybe have one of the best results in my department? Then, rather than describing or introducing myself in an unspecified way, I sincerely liked the way that my achievements portrayed me. These achievements allowed me to introduce myself to people even before they got to see me. In that way, I ensured that I was always better than I was last year or far better off than my last achievement.

Many people focus on competition with other people rather than focusing more on self-competition, which is far better and more productive to self-actualization than competing with others (i.e. self-competition is dependent on past achievements and not just other people's achievements).

Analyse your competition wisely and you will not be competing wrongly.

Action plan for self-competition

Step 1: Test yourself daily and try to outscore your previous highest performance/score.

Step 2: Expand your focus on a daily basis.

Step 3: Look out for the best in your specialty and make that your stepping stone.

Step 4: Challenge the experts to recognize the level which you are at now.

Step 5: Make a commitment to do more today than you did yesterday.

Step 6: Use your failures as your stepping stone, learn from them and don't be discouraged.

Step 7: Understand that you have no boundary except the one that you create for yourself.

When you engage in the above activities, you may find that they will help you boost your self-competitiveness. When done on a weekly basis, you will get used to them and before long you will realize that you have repeated them 52 times in a year.

If you are committed to this simple but effective ways of building your self-competitiveness, you may find that something has been shifted inside of you and that a new 'you' may have just been created.

Self Innovation and Creativity

Innovation is an act of thinking and acting differently, while creativity occurs when you bring something new into existence; how, therefore, can you be more innovative and creative by yourself?

> *Innovation is capable of being presented as a discipline, capable of being learned, capable of being practiced. Entrepreneurs need to search purposefully for the sources of innovation, the changes and their symptoms that indicate opportunities for successful innovation.* (Drucker, 1985)

These are some of the processes and skills that will be discussed as part of the SIM activities.

Innovation and creativity are skills that can be taught, learnt and practised. In as much as they can be learnt, it shows that even if you were never innovative before, you can now observe how innovators think and act.

Although other skills can be improved upon, it is possible for you to work on your innovation skills by applying these four crucial steps:

i. **Visualization**: This involves seeing beyond the present situation or circumstances. It takes discipline in order to look at something differently when everyone else is looking in another direction. Until they see or meet their expectations, only a dedicated person may determine to look at a different direction or angle. Visualization goes beyond the naked eyes and it requires the mind to paint a picture that can only be achieved when one communicates it to the executors and that is what self-innovation is all about. While visualization is done single-handedly, the execution can be achieved or realized by many people.

ii. **Visitation**: Innovation comes by visiting great places that will expand our minds into seeing new perspectives and embracing new cultures or habits, which invariably affect our thinking and the way we see things. Indirectly, we begin to see something new or different from a usual occurrence.

iii. **Valuation:** One of the main problems with self-innovation is the lack of commitment and this can occur when one does not value his or her innovation skills or has doubts about what the mind has been able to picture. I agree that there may be doubt when one conceptualizes an idea; however, letting the doubt settle is an unwise thing to do, simply because it devalues the concept of thinking about that idea and it can also reduce the passion for self-innovation, which can make a person feel as if they are a failure.

iv. **Verification:** With every innovation, there must be a time for verification. If we are to achieve a thorough self-innovation, we must sincerely verify our findings and cultivate the habit of asking questions that can generate an answer to unravel more findings. The process of verification in self-innovation is vital because with many questions we are already drawing closer to the answer or solution to the problem: that is why we must always verify our findings if we want to improve our self-innovation skills.

In order to make it easier to remember, I have chosen the letters that start with V so that it will be easier to remember these steps as the key factors to increasing our self-innovation skills.

According to Gregersen, Dyer and Christensen (2011) innovators think differently and self-innovation is possible if you can simply ask yourself the following *five diagnostic questions* to test your DNA and see if there's need for you to improve your innovation skills:

i. *Associational thinking*: We tend to be more innovative when we are around those people who are thinking like us (i.e. birds of a feather flock together).

   "A dream you dream alone is only a dream but a dream you dream together is reality." (Lennon, 1940–1980) That means that one can choose to increase his or her self-innovation by associating with great thinkers of great things. It is a choice, so choose wisely. Do you think like great inventors or great innovators?

ii. *Questioning*: As we have said previously, asking the right questions increases your level of self-innovation and makes you come across as relevant or irreplaceable.

   "You can tell whether a man is clever by his answers and you can equally tell whether a man is wise by his questions." (Mahfouz, 1911–2006)

   Are you inquisitive or do you challenge the status quo?

iii. *Observing*: In order to gather the requirements for solving a problem, we need to critically observe what the actual problem is and what potential solutions would be ideal or suitable for solving the problem, before we begin to implement those solutions, one after the other. Observation can be done randomly but individual opinions may have to be considered, hence the reason for self-innovation.

How observant are you in finding out new things and unravelling new products or services?

iv. *Networking*: It is a personal choice whether or not to discuss ideas with people. Such deliberations may help to foster increased self-innovation in us. We have to withdraw from our comfort zones and share ideas with people, solely for the purpose of making these ideas and concepts a reality. In an atmosphere where there is the opportunity to network, it is great to network with people who share a similar interest with us and this can help us unravel the mystery behind the execution of our great ideas.

Do you mingle or socialize with people of like minds in order to share great insights?

v. *Experimenting*: With experimenting on an idea that has just been generated, it may be impossible to determine whether the idea can be used or not. The purpose of experimenting is to shed more light on a hidden treasure in the form of ideas. This light is used to understand the idea more and endeavour to find the best way possible to make it a reality.

Are you curious to find out new things and generate reports on your findings?

This quote from a veteran innovation leader explains what self-innovation is all about: *"Innovation distinguishes between a leader and a follower."* (Jobs, 1955–2011)

If you want to be a leader in your industry or market, improve your self-innovation skills and it will pay out by increasing your brand recognition and turnover.

Action plan for self-innovation and creativity

Step 1: Always think outside the box.

Step 2: Change your attitude by finding reasons why things can work before they can't.

Step 3: Eliminate assumption, limiting beliefs and preoccupations that are holding you back.

Step 4: Widen your horizon by trying new things, read things outside your specialty and see things from outside of your view or environment.

Step 5: Don't get stuck in one frame of mind, but be open-minded and flexible to adapt to changes.

Step 6: Recognize when you've been creative in the past and pick moments when you had good ideas and realize what you have done well before.

Step 7: Go beyond the obvious and try to find other ways of doing what you do now.

Step 8: Come up with at least 10 random but constructive ideas daily.

Step 9: Stimulate your mind by getting your brain to keep flowing and keep your mental health in shape.

Step 10: Make an 'I did' list.

Step 11: Hang out with people who are smarter.

Step 12: Do something scary by pushing yourself a little further.

Step 13: Play 'smart' games like chess and scrabble to help you expand your mind.

Step 14: End the day with a 'playback' for reflection on your daily achievements.

Self-Valuation

Value is not bought but earned. A person is valued not by what he or she gets but by what he or she gives. Value is synonymous with worth and self-valuation; it goes beyond the ordinary sense of knowing about self, yet understanding that we are desirable by other people.

If I sincerely know my worth, I will know what I should be involved with and what I should not be entangled with. I have battled with self-valuation for many years until recently I decided to figure out why I've been treated in that way. First, it was my inability to fight back or defend myself when I was faced with people who wanted to take me for granted. This attitude continued for many years until I realized that I only just needed to state my mind and leave these people with their options of what I'd said. It was only then that I stopped bothering about what people thought about me or about what I said. I also came to realize that they didn't even care about me in the first place. Why then did I care about what they felt or about what they said? It was only then that it dawned on me that I needed to value myself, especially what came out of my mouth before others might begin to value me. When someone wants to sincerely contribute to what you're saying, they will do that genuinely and not sarcastically. If, on the other hand, they have no value for you, it is because you have shown yourself as a person of low self-value or they've decided not to assume any kind of value to your personality.

Gold is a scarce metal. I can only conclude that gold is very expensive because it is scarce and rare to find, and this naturally places value on any gold if it's identified as the real metal. According to Wikipedia website: *"The value of gold is rooted in its medium rarity, easily handling, easy smelting, non-corrosiveness, distinct colour and non-reactiveness to other elements and these qualities cannot be found in most of the other metals."* (Wikipedia, 1976)

The value placed on something determines how people will relate and respond to that entity, which is the same for every human being. If we identify the value that we carry as individuals and we can communicate that value to others, who relate to us on a regular basis, then that value will have a great effect on how people will relate to us – and how much value they place on us and our relationship with them.

"Change is hard because people overestimate the value of what they have and they underestimate the value of what they may gain by giving up what they have." (Belasco and Stayer, 1993)

Action plan for self-valuation

Step 1: Celebrate the little successes of today because they increase your hope for the future.

Step 2: Strive to be better than most people if not all.

Step 3: Rate yourself in your areas of interest and develop on that.

Step 4: What is worth doing is worth doing well, so be excellent at what you do.

Step 5: I must feel important with myself before others will accept me.

Step 6: You cannot value others if you don't value yourself.

Step 7: Listen to suggestions but respect your own decisions.

Self Preparation for Leadership.

Leaders are made, and they can be made just like everybody else. However, the quality of the preparation for leadership will determine whether a leader will be effective or otherwise. This SIM manual can identify those skills that would help anyone who desires to be an effective leader, and it'll start preparing them for the task ahead.

Preparing for leadership simply means that long before you even become a leader, you are already getting ready for a leadership role by identifying those things that qualify you for a leadership position.

We shall be mentioning some of these qualities shortly. In as much as this manual is not about leadership, we must be rest assured that everything revolves round leadership and we are consciously or unconsciously leading someone, somewhere by either our thoughts or actions.

Preparing yourself for that task will take determination, concentration; moreover, you will require energy and stamina that will allow you to experience things that can make you become a leader. Self Identification Management provides the understanding that you must first identify yourself as a leader, even before it eventually manifests on the outside or when you finally get to be accepted as a leader. This self-awareness creates inside of you the notion that you already have the capacity to become a leader, and these kinds of qualities will indirectly push you to become a leader. A sincere leader does not reveal that he or she is a leader because what they do is more important than what they say; such leaders are categorized as Servant Leaders, because their main focus is to lead their followers through effective services, while others emulate them. Besides, service is the act of delivering or adding value to the lives of other people through problem-solving.

Therefore, a Servant Leader is someone who delivers value to other people and he or she influences them to do likewise to other people. A Servant Leader must be an influencer and they must influence people directly or indirectly. It is the goodwill of those you are leading and not your own selfish interest that is most important for influencing people.

The sixth President of the United States of America described self-preparation for leadership:

"If your actions inspire others to dream more, learn more, do more and to become more, you are a leader." (Adams, 1767–1848)

Regarding self-preparation for leadership, an effective leader must possess certain qualities and the following are some of these:

- Decision-making
- Risk-taking
- Influential qualities
- Negotiation skills
- Courage and boldness
- Analytical skills
- People management
- Listening skills
- Learning wisely

In an ideal world, a good leader must be able to make sound judgements or decisions that can positively affect his or her followers and this involves having deep passion for other individuals. A leader who doesn't have any real connection with his or her followers will not think of them before taking risks, even if the risks taken produces a negative outcome.

Realistically, people want to see you doing something reasonably well before they come to join you; people may sacrifice their own goals in order to fulfil yours as their leader. That is why we must courageously influence our followers positively so that they can be motivated to see us through to the outcome of our goals as leaders. Listening to our followers is equivalent to finding out whether our actions are productive or ineffective.

A leader envisions a destination; then he or she begins to work towards communicating to those people who will help or assist him or her to getting there. Before calling on other people to go on a journey, a leader must first identify where the journey is leading to. That, in essence, is why SIM practices must be adhere to, before commencing the journey to fulfil the vision.

"It is the willingness and capacity to develop their skills that differentiate leaders from their followers." (Bennis and Nanus, 1985)

For instance, let's take the story of the lion being the king of the jungle. Is it true that the lion can rule over all other animals in the jungle or that the lion is stronger than all other animals out there? We shall briefly list some of the reasons why we have consciously and unconsciously accepted this story without analyzing how it has evolved over the years.

Ordinarily, lions are bold with confidence and they possess this pride that makes them behave in such a boastful way; however, they have a soft side as well because they don't just go hunting unless they are hungry. That means that when another animal is roaming about, it is possible that this animal goes free without being hurt or killed by the lion; I found this to be strange. Furthermore, we know that lions have a strategy for hunting and it's so special that they have to keep on hunting in that way if they truly want to get food to eat and they pass on this knowledge unto their younger ones. Let's not forget that it is the lioness (female) that actually does the hunting while the lion (male) remains at their territory to secure the home and cubs (if any) against the enemies. When a pride of lions and lionesses want to dominate an area or a portion of the forest, they do this by carefully inspecting the area and they demarcate or select their own portion of the forest by urinating around where they have dominated; then they announce their occupancy of that area by roaring loudly for other animals, within a five-mile radius, to be aware that they have claimed and taken possession of that portion of the forest, so no other animal should trespass. Isn't that a relaxed way to scare people away from their possessions? These traits allow the lion and lioness to gain any kingdom that they may desire to possess. In addition, they believe that they are capable of hunting down any kind of animal except venomous snakes and tough-skinned crocodiles; hence they portray themselves as leaders of the jungle.

From the story of the lion as the king of the jungle, we can see that lions have identified what it takes to possess a kingdom and they portray themselves as the leaders of the jungle. While other animals have accepted this, it will be like that until other animals stand up to defend this theory. We human beings ought to learn one or two things from this analogy – we can identify those traits that make us unique and that make people accept whatever we call ourselves to them and not what they choose to call us. If we have identified ourselves and understand those things that make us stand out, then people will accept us for who we portray that we are.

In general, influencers are leaders, but unconsciously they may not be aware that they are leaders until they can find someone who can help them to figure out what they are doing as influencers, that is, captivating and influencing others. We all have different ways that we influence people (directly or indirectly). People take it upon themselves to identify what exactly they are doing that is making others follow them: thus, they have been able to identify themselves in order to present themselves effectively to the general populace and this would also allow them to be able to figure out more key strengths about themselves that they can leverage on.

Action plan for self-preparation for leadership

Step 1: Read great books that expand your knowledge about your vision.

Step 2: Listen carefully and learn something new on a daily basis.

Step 3: Inspire and motivate at least one person daily.

Step 4: Influence some positivism today.

Step 5: Build other people to build other people today.

Step 6: Build great relationships with people by serving them genuinely.

Step 7: Envision great things today.

Self-Execution.

A self-executive person is known to be an independent person. They come across as confident in whatever they do because they always evaluate before they follow any idea that might cross their minds.

We've discussed the DNA of an innovator while explaining self-innovation and creativity. However, self-innovators can only be responsible for the beginning of any innovation process and, in due course, we would need to execute innovative ideas, services or products and this is where we need executors (i.e. those who have developed adequate self-execution skills.)

Executors are not only good at reviewing ideas for innovation, but they actually follow the idea through to implementation. They are not just observers of innovative ideas but executors of these great ideas. When we talk of executors, we mean individuals who make a non-realistic idea become realistic. They may not understand the source of the idea, but they are willing to do more to bring something of substance out of that idea. They may not be good at coming up with innovative ideas, but they can make a virtual substance (innovative idea) become a real product or an enhanced service.

We cannot talk of self-innovators without acknowledging that other people are also actually responsible for implementing those ideas in order to get to the completion stage. In the process of completing the cycle of innovation, we will identify skill sets for an executor to successfully bring an innovative idea to completion.

Ideally, there are many ways to develop the skills that qualify someone to be categorized as a self-executor. The most important consideration, however, is the process of testing to identify whether that person truly possesses the skills of a self-executor or not. According to Gregersen and Dyer (2013) this list of four skills will match the kind of skills that an ideal self-executor should possess:

i. *Analyzing:* This involves a lot of research, observation and verification of your findings before you proceed to development. A self-executor must be willing to analyse his or her findings, and to prove whether he or she has succeeded in recording a breakthrough of an achievement.

ii. *Planning:* Thorough planning precedes any successful project or activity and without detailed planning, it may take longer to execute the task or you may not get any result. It is burdensome and complicated when you get to the end of a task before you realize that you actually left something very important undone, just because you didn't plan the project/ task very well. This is what can happen when you overlook the importance of planning and overestimate the hassle that can be avoided through proper planning.

iii. *Detail-oriented:* Every detail counts and every count is collected for the purpose of making decisions. The details of any task given to a self-executor have to be accurate; otherwise it may not authenticate the essence of executing the task in the first place. Therefore, the self-executor needs to identify the details of the project or task before embarking on it.

iv. *Self-discipline:* Discipline precedes success and one needs to be disciplined in one way or the other in order to achieve success in anything they do. If you don't have self-discipline as a self-executor, it simply means that you may not be committed to the task you're handling or you may not be able to deliver an exceptional outcome for that task. This is regrettable for many people who think that their skills as self-executors may not resolve the level of the outcome of their tasks.

If the level of self-discipline that you have as a self-executor is not in proportion to the task you're handling, it will reflect in your work and in the product of your implementation.

Now that we have identified the skills set for self-execution, we should try to assess ourselves against all these skills and verify if we truly have the trait of self-execution because we are the chief executors of our own individual destinies.

Action plan for self-execution

Step 1: Encourage yourself to always take bold steps daily in doing things.

Step 2: Dish it and 'just do it' (Nike's slogan).

Step 3: Understand it enough before you execute it enough.

Step 4: For anything to happen to me, I must give my consent to it.

Step 5: I have to control myself to control any other thing out there. My self-control affects other controls.

Step 6: I must account for my own fortune or misfortune; no one lives my life for me.

Step 7: You must know where you're going before others can help you to get there.

Step 8: Make your hourly/daily/weekly/monthly/yearly plans unique and they will reflect the type of person you are.

Self-Actualization.

People would know that you truly understand yourself when they can see you living the life of a self-actualized person. That's the moment when it doesn't really matter if people are aware of who you are or what you look like; but when your name is being mentioned, people begin to say excellent things about you, whereas there would be at least one person who would want to say bad things about you. The most important aspect of self-actualization is that after you've fully identified your true 'self' and decided to manage that 'self' to become a self-actualized person, you have actually not tried to do things in the way that would please people, but in the way that you think might make you achieve actualization. This point is almost the final goal that we all need to experience before we exit this world; essentially, many people will read this book and still not believe that they can actually achieve the level of self-actualization.

You don't have to be in a particular age bracket before you can fully achieve your potential but you must start somewhere. This, in fact, is the identification of that self in you. The illustration about these two words (*selfish* and *selfless*) should provide us some understanding about what we hope to achieve by discussing self-identification management in respect of self-actualization. A selfish person makes himself or herself the top priority of everything, while a selfless person thinks more of others than anything else. When we look closely at these two words *selfish* and *selfless*, we will discover that they both start with self with the addition of other words -*ish* and -*less*, respectively. The only thing that both these words (i.e. selfish and selfless) have in common is self; which means that when we're unable to identify that something called self exist, then it may not be possible to actualize either the selfish or selfless desire; This is my own little explanation on how to demonstrate the importance of self in all aspects of our lives. One key benefit of a self-actualized life is that you impact lives with your gifts and talents, to the point where values are added to people who come in contact with you (directly or indirectly) because then you are committed to delivering a service to them and not the other way round. People know when you are genuinely interested in them and they know when you partially care for them because of the benefits that you derive from serving them. A self-actualized life means that you live for others and not for yourself, which invariably means that you must have lived a life of legacy that touches others. Riches come with their own benefits if they're used for a good cause.

According to Maslow (1987) self-actualization is *"the final level of psychological development that can be achieved when all basic and mental needs are essentially fulfilled and the actualization of the full personal potential takes place."*

In his theory, we can deduce that Maslow studied the reactions of people and how they are motivated towards these needs. Maslow also understood that people desire several needs; the need of self-actualization, however, is the most critical one achieved by very few people and this is because few actually believe that they can achieve Maslow's hierarchy of needs. Maslow simply focused more on the potentials of the human race and how to fulfil such potentials, rather than worrying why people do not achieve their needs at this stage. It also follows that Maslow understood that human beings have the power and enablement to achieve this stage of self-actualization if they can connect their energy to the purpose of this cause, implying that one must go through rigorous self-motivation before they can get to the point of believing that this is possible.

A self-actualized person is one who understands the needs of fulfilling his or her highest potentials. What, it may be asked, happens to those who do not even believe or have any idea that they have potential? That is why I believe that the most important and essential responsibility of every individual is to identify their true 'self' and begin to live for it by managing it effectively.

How then should you meet your needs if you don't know them or you've not even identified that you have a need?

Living a self-actualized life is such a difficult decision and one must be really dedicated to fulfilling that purpose: a life like that does not come randomly or mistakenly but will require rigorous preparation and planning. Discipline is also involved in the process of self-actualization: a disciplined person is almost as committed to their purpose of living as a life-and-death situation. Hence this quote, *"What a man can be, he must be."*

Action plan for self-actualization

Step 1: Understand that there is a need and this need must be fulfilled.

Step 2: Commit yourself to executing at least one thing at a time, then progress from there.

Step 3: Make it a necessity to increase or improve in at least one aspect of your life daily.

Step 4: Create a maximum height that you think you can achieve and then follow suit.

Step 5: Make all your achievements a stepping stone to your next level of achievement.

Step 6: Bring positivity to your actualization by speaking positively to yourself.

Step 7: Narrow down the most important thing to you as you swim ahead in the game of life.

Step 8: Plan forwards, fall forwards, reflect backwards, think ahead; and above all, move ahead.

CONCLUSION

If you've been following this book from the beginning, by now you should've been able to adhere to some of the instructions and practices stated here; furthermore, you would concur with the author that it is necessary to identify your true 'self' before working out how to fully manage it in order to be rewarded with a fulfilling life. To conclude this discussion, I would like to draw your attention to the hardest yet most rewarding aspect of SIM; this may not work for everybody, but it is definitely going to work for anyone who wants to be remembered as a person of substantial value to their environment, society, location, nation or even the world at large.

You will be remembered for what you give and not what you receive. The level at which people will remember you is dependent on the level at which you've given yourself to them. I will give a few examples that will help to ascertain that it's really more rewarding to give than to receive, though it is not a crime to receive from people. When a person with no children dies, and he or she has never done anything that is meaningful for people to remember them, then automatically it's easier for people to just bury the person and afterwards forget that they ever existed; however, if he or she had a child, people can look at the face of the child and remember that the parent of the child once lived, before they could give birth to this child. This is one of the ways of giving something to people so that they can remember you, but if you're unable to bear a child before death comes, then it would be expected that you touch so many lives so that even if you don't live behind a child, they can easily use the memory of positive things that you've done for them to remember you and appreciate that they have experienced you in one way or the other. Either ways, it is very advisable that we touch as many lives as possible while we're here on earth, because this will speak for us while we're gone.

The following is another example of giving ourselves for the cause of making life better for others. Any seed that wants to become a big tree in the future must first give itself up to be buried or planted in the soil. In due course the seed will spring up out of the soil to grow up and become a big tree that can sustain many people. It's a sign of dedication that seeds can give themselves up to be planted in the soil and then sprout out to support those people who bury them in the soil. Farmers do not care too much whether the dead seed survives or not, but what they naturally think about more is that the small seeds they planted are able to grow up and feed many people in order for them to achieve their aim. These seeds must give themselves up to be planted in the soil and die before they can then sprout out again for the farmers to harvest them. It is a difficult and delicate situation, but the result is that human beings and even some animals cannot live without these small seeds that naturally give themselves up for us to be fed. That alone is a sign of sacrifice and we human beings also have to sacrifice something whereby others can live; and, as a consequence, they tend to constantly remember us for our great sacrifice. These tasks are only possible when our SIM has been accomplished and we strictly adhere to its plan of execution.

How many people really know the capacity of the palm tree and what it can give us? Because of the many benefits of the palm tree we should never forget its existence. As we begin to analyse the importance of the palm trees that we have in our gardens or farms, we observe that this tree yields assets that can provide food or that can enhance our cooking and meals; at the same time, some of its branches are important sources of wood for building strong houses, furniture making, roofing houses, oil making, paper making and wine making. These are just a few of the numerous things that can be derived from what the palm tree gives us as human beings. Therefore, we should respect this tree, which is more valuable than some of the other trees in the forest. In many instances, we don't even know the names of other trees because we've never benefitted from them, or we simply assume that we can never achieve anything from them; hence we assume we don't need to know anything about them.

There is an aspect of giving that sounds very difficult to understand – the aspect of giving your *self*. You must first identify your *self* before you can give. The well-known saying says *"giving is better than receiving"*, although we mostly receive more than we give. It is not right or wrong to receive more than we give, but it's just that we have programmed our minds to always receive, rather than to give more than we receive. I can guarantee you that many of us receive more than we actually give. This is not simply because we don't want to give – it is because we've not understood the practices of giving long enough that we no longer think about giving before we actually give. When it becomes a habit and a commitment to keep giving, only then will it be enjoyable to give more than to receive more. Here are some questions:

What exactly are we giving? Service

Why are we giving what we give? At our discretion, but it's extremely rewarding in the long run

And to whom do we actually give? Environment, humankind and the plant/animal kingdom

These are some of the many questions that may run through our minds when we ponder on what to give. The SIM manual encourages us to give in order to release our own selves to become a tool that will serve others rather than being served. Service is one of the many things that we must give. We must be serviceable enough so that others can see us being helpful to them when they need help. The service implied here is not the flimsy kind of service that is prevalent at working places now, where people only concentrate on eye service, but that dedicated type of service that goes beyond mere words and that's purposely directed to win people over to the attention of your service. Service is not only about what you have; it's about what you give and how you give it. If you're really dedicated to giving yourself to others, you would not lack what to give and that means you wouldn't lack what you want because what you want is what you will give anyway. For example, if you're hungry and do not have food to eat but eventually someone gives you food to eat. If afterwards, you see someone else that need food, you'll be encouraged to want to give the person food, if you do have because you now know how it feels to be hungry. This may look like a complicated theory because people don't seem to understand that they get back what they have actually given. Sometimes it can be difficult for people to know that it is what they gave will be what they receive back.

In other words, it is very difficult to get a reward without some form of sacrifice involved. If we agree on this principle, then we should also know that people will not reward us for anything else other than our sacrifices.

You have not really achieved much if people only appreciate you when you are alive. The great level of appreciation comes when an individual is dead because then it is clear that the person has really influenced his or her world positively by living a sacrificial life. From the beginning of this book, we've been talking about identifying self; we are concluding by saying that, based on the understanding of what we know about our self, now is the time to give our 'self'. Although all of us should not give ourselves to benefit other people in the same way, the most critical consideration is that we are at least giving something in one way or the other. Giving can be accomplished in many ways, such as time, talent, riches, encouragement, hope, motivation, energy, leadership and administration skills. The basic principle of giving of ourselves is a function of how much we love people and how much we care to see this world as a better place even after we have died. Love is a powerful emotion, and in some ways, it's been represented as death because when you truly love a person, then you become vulnerable and you want to die for the person or people you acclaim to love. Genuine love is not only proven through death but that is one of the ways in which love can be shown. For example, Nelson Mandela went to prison because he was fighting for the freedom of his people and that alone made his people like, respect and honour him for his bravery. Jesus Christ also died for the sins of the world, although so many people are still in doubt of this truth, but we Christians know in our hearts that this is true. Also, in the movie *Titanic* where Jack Dawson died for his love, Rose DeWitt Bukater. It's not only through death that you can show your love for others: dying for the people you love is a crucial way of showing that you can do anything for them.

Giving must be done voluntarily and genuinely, not because we are expecting someone or people to give something back to us, but because we care enough to give ourselves for them. It is not only the human race that we can give ourselves to. We can also give ourselves and our time to the plant and animal kingdom, whereby animals are treated fairly by every organism and they don't emerge as preys to those organisms that are predators.

Law of completion

This law states that *"you are not complete yet until you give yourself completely to selflessness."*

In the real world, people do not remember you for what you did for yourself or what you accumulated for yourself – they are more concerned about what you did for others. Although it is possible that people may not even show the gratitude of what you did for them while you are still alive, they will surely remember these things when you are dead.

Law of giving

This law states that *"you should give like you never gave before so that you can receive like you never received before."*

The fundamental truth about living an effective life is to be remembered for greatness; and greatness comes when you've done something great such as giving yourself for others. Greedy people only live for themselves, whereas a self-fulfilling and self-rewarding life can be pursued continually for the benefit of others and for the good of every living creature.

REFERENCES

Adams J.Q. (1767–1848) American statesman and sixth President of the United States (1825–1829).

Aristotle (382–322 BC) *The basic works of Aristotle* (McKeon R. ed., 2001) Modern Library, Random House Publishing Group: New York.

Belasco J.A. and Stayer R. (1993) *Flight of the buffalo: Soaring to excellence, learning to let employees lead.* Warner Books: New York.

Bennis W.G. and Nanus B. (1985) *Leaders: The strategies for taking charge.* Harper & Row: New York.

Dawson J. (1892–1912) protagonist in the *Titanic*; lost in the *Titanic* disaster of 1912; his love Rose DeWitt Bukater survived and lived to be 101.

Demp B. (2014) *The quotable coach: Daily nuggets of practical wisdom.* CreateSpace Independent Publishing Platform (part of Amazon group).

Dorfman H.A. (2002) *The mental ABCs of pitching: A handbook for performance enhancement.* Diamond Communications: Lanham, Maryland.

Dorfman H.A. and Kuehl K. (2002) *The mental game of baseball: A guide to peak performance.* Diamond Communications: Lanham, Maryland.

Drucker P.F. (1985) *Innovation and entrepreneurship: Practice and principles.* Harper & Row: New York.

Gregersen H., Dyer J. and Christensen C.M. (2011) *The innovator's DNA: Mastering the five skills of disruptive innovators.* Harvard Business Press: Boston, Mass.

Gregersen H. and Dyer J. (2013) The secret to unleashing genius. *Forbes.* 192(3): 96–108.

Hoffman R. (1967–) American internet entrepreneur and co-founder of Linkedin.

Jobs S. (1955–2011) American entrepreneur, inventor, chairman and CEO of Apple Inc.

Krieger R.A. (2002) *Civilization's quotations: Life's ideal.* Algora Pub: New York.

Lao-tzu (604–531 BC) legendary Chinese philosopher in the sixth century.

La Rochefoucauld F. (1900) *Reflections: Or, sentences and moral maxims.* H.M. Caldwell: New York.

Leading thoughts: Building a community of leaders "Quotes on self discipline" (1996–2003). Available from http://www.leadershipnow.com/disciplinequotes.html [accessed 01/02/2014]

Lennon J. (1940–1980) singer, songster and founder of the Beatles Rock group.

Lincoln A. (1809–1865) American statesman and 16th President of the United States (1861–1865); assassinated after the end of the American Civil War.

Mahfouz N. (1911–2006) Egyptian novelist and winner of the Nobel Prize for Literature in 1988.

Mandela N. (1918–2013) First black president of South Africa (1994–1999); Nobel Prize for peace 1993; imprisoned in South Africa (1963–1989).

Maslow A.H. (1987) *Maslow's hierarchy of needs*. Salenger: Santa Monica CA.

Maxwell J.C. (2013) *Sometimes you win – sometimes you learn: Life's greatest lessons are gained from our losses*. Center Street: New York.

Maxwell J.C. (2003) *Attitude 101: What every leader needs to know*. Nelson Publishers: Nashville TN.

New Oxford Dictionary of English (1998) Oxford University Press: Oxford, UK.

Oyediran T. (2013) Teesoft: Motivation. Weblog (September 30, 2013). Available from http://tee-soft.blogspot.co.uk/2013/09/motivation.html

Oyediran T. (2014) Teesoft: Competitive Analysis. Weblog (May 21, 2014). Available from http://tee-soft.blogspot.co.uk/2014/05/competitive-analysis.html

Priestley D. (2010) *Become a key person of influence (KPI): 5 step sequence to becoming one of the most highly valued and highly paid people in your industry*. Ecademy Press: St Albans, UK.

Wikipedia (1976) Gold. Available from http://en.wikipedia.org/wiki/Gold [accessed 27/02/2015].